I'll Be Home Late Tonight

Thomas McAfee

I'll Be Home Late Tonight   *Poems*

University of Missouri Press • Columbia, Missouri

Some of these poems have been published previously.
They are included in this collection by permission
of the publishers of *The Carleton Miscellany*, *The
Colorado Quarterly*, *Contact*, *FOCUS/Midwest*, *Inscape*,
The Kansas City Star, *Midwestern University Quarterly*,
Northwest Review, *The Poetry Bag*, *The St. Louis Post-
Dispatch*, *The Transatlantic Review*, and *The University
Review*.

"My Lady of the Black Raincoat" has been published,
in an earlier version, in *The Girl in the Black Raincoat*,
edited by George Garrett. It appears here by permission
of the publishers, Duell, Sloan & Pearce.

FOR MIRIAM

Contents

Contents

Contents

PART ONE

EXTREME UNCTION: ACT THREE

I think you've gone the limit,
love, throwing glasses,
shooting off
at the mouth,
parading yourself
and myself, too,
to the wide wide world.
— Do your jungle duties
at home, where the flushing's loud
and no one can hear you yell.
— And keep all your minor
jealousy
in the cage of your own
sullen self.
— First thing, and last,
don't call me up
at some swank hour,
like noon,
to apologize.

The bitch is at her business again,
pretending:
she is the King of Gibraltar's mistress;
she drove a Ford for Al Capone.

I don't know a single respectable tree —
oak, pine, maple —
that would let her stand beneath it
more than a minute.

COMPLAINT

Why does she strut so
when she's so bored?
tossing away a cigarette.
Well, she wasn't meant for oblivion.

THE WAY IT HAS TO BE
— for Dean Swift

If we could remove ourselves to scented groves,
Away from the racket of flushing toilets,
From belching after beer, from coughing . . .

If we could conjure our stink away,
Make pure as poems our rotting teeth
And breathe sweetly sweetly to our loves . . .

Dean Swift, another bath is necessary!
The conjugal bed must be perfumed.
Meat for the soul has to ripen.

The sea will not hold still,
Not even when,
Smooth as woman-thigh skin,
It deceives the brain in the eye
And moves perfectly into sky.

The sea will not hold still,
And neither will you, my dear.
You lie asleep but still I hear
Your run-away voice running on,
Bitchily or in love song.

The sea will not hold still,
And I would have it this way
With you as with sea. God keep the day
When you might sit at the window,
Quiet and unmoving,
And be still forever to my loving.

I lay
In a tangle of graves
Till that sweet instant
When our spirits mixed.

At this,
Earth was fixed
Beneath the root
Of a hickory tree.

Oranges were edible;
Death, an institute.
We were total undoing.
Love was no more a pursuit

Than the hummingbird's
Or the red bird's
Or the starling's.
Love went without words

At all.
Adam's fall
Was there already.
So was Eve's.

I DON'T MIND CRYING BUT . . .

*The great advantage of a hotel is that
it's a refuge from home life.*

When the elevator busted
I was there
And more certainly
you were there.
We were characters
in a movie, almost,
and longing for ground
and the sound of somebody
without our sound.

We made it, love,
for a little while,
and didn't break.

In the lobby,
we saw our mistake was good.
You made it straight
for cigarettes —
and I for that awful
revolving door.

You take the cherry from
this sweaty glass,
and remember
I'll be here, almost,
I imagine,
this time of year, next year,
in these linen precincts,
but you won't — ever —
you won't even round up
the music.
That's growing, my darling.

You are swarming like bees.
I can't afford such terrible
sound without meaning.

ON A PAINTING

They live in a world of pink and pink,
One light, one going peach.
They play strange ball, they syncopate,
They nod each to each.

Four with no faces, four with no air,
They range from blue to red.
Their world is never anywhere,
And yet they are not dead.

One ball is square, one like an egg.
How will the bouncing go?
Skywards? or against a leg?
No one will ever know.

Of games and players I prefer
This game of static motion,
These players who will not defer
To any commotion.

Q: "HOW CAN YOU BEAT DIAMONDS?"
    —from an ad in *Life* magazine

A: Almost any way you choose.
   By not confusing them with polished
   cherry wood, or with the gleam
   in a doe's eye.
      They may lend esteem
   to the wrinkle or the vein of your
   mistress' hand; but do not confuse
   them with the running waters
   of her heart.
                  Jewels are less
   than art; witless; far less
   than the ruining body's
   seizures.
                  They last forever.
   But they are better as metaphor
   than real.

FOR THE MARRIAGE
—for Gail and R. P. Dickey

May the green light
Shine. May the banners
At the filling station wave.
May the pavement be
Fresh paved.
It is not fitting I
Should offer benediction.
I do not. I say,
May all the cars roar for you.

Why name her except Blood and Earth
or perhaps Church Stone
or Bone Marrow?
She will arrive sadly
at what she is and who
she is: Sparrow Bone,
Cherry Pit.   — Once, lingering
in cool river water, she will
come to it, seize her name . . .
— No matter the tag-plate
you weary her neck with, she
will forgive — if she will —
what you have summoned her to.
— She will name herself
for some unheard-of flower,
in the woods, by a brook,
protected by ferns.

DESPEDIDA

after Lorca (for James Miles)

The day I die
leave the casket
open.

The boy
across the street
is eating grapes.

(I see him
from my window
now.)

The reaper
always reaps
the wheat.

(I hear him
from my window
now.)

The day I die
leave the casket
open!

The Spanish have words for dying
More conservative and far
More festive than ours.
   We must put the act
In terms of bankers and bricklayers
And baseball players.
   You can see those banners on those faces.
They are solemn banners
Saying, I'm complete, I'm complete.
   Even at morning, over
Hearty coffee,
Our heroic men, just waking up,
Have that silver dollar look
In both the eyes.
   The Spanish seem to think of yesterday,
And late last night,
The wine still purple on their lips.
   That's the difference, I suppose:
The going into something with one's wine;
The falling out of something where the silver was.

EL NIÑO LOCO
   after Lorca

I nodded good afternoon,
but it was not afternoon:
it was midnight last night
and midnight yesterday morning.

The afternoon was shrugged away
like dreaming.

(What is the use of nodding?
It is the dark of moon
last night.)

He is in lunar bronze.
I am the one waiting.

— suggested by the Portuguese "Autopsicografia"
of Fernando Pessoa (*Poesias*, 1958)

Deluding himself,
the Magician,
for he feigns
his metaphors out of a hat . . .

Reader — out there
in the darkness — your hell
is real
and lovely just once.

His hell is once but twice.
Your hell is once but never.

Call it the top of the head . . .
Disguise it as spirit . . .
It's a hat of rabbit
tricks on stage.

Dead is like the hammer
Hitting the nail
Into the stone.
It is like belief
In bone,
Without flesh.
It is like virgins
Keeping on.

For twenty years my good wife gave
Me dinner at just seven.
Then she was dinner in the grave
Scarce soul had got to Heaven.

ATHLETE

He moves to the music of his body,
Courts a mirror like a steady date. He moves
Under a censored sky of despair.
Nobody else — nobody, anywhere —
Could know such grief and green exultation
As he, watching the muscle and bone decline.
And nobody else could smudge out so well
The empty stadium's lime goal line.

SKULL PRACTICE

In mind, bent for the scrimmage,
and in body, relaxed,
we watch the chalk
slide its way on the slate.
The coach groans on
about arrows and Jesus
and winning.
                    It is truly
skull practice. I know
by heart my plays.
But what will happen
to this art I've perfected
when those other skulls,
perfected too, thud
against mine
and redefine these obviously
infallible rules?

The car had turned over.
My face pressed against the window.
The window was close
to the red clay bank, ragged
with wet green weeds.
It was still raining. And the water
made bloody rivulets.
I noticed the frond of a weed
dripping water.
I said, "It's a Japanese drawing."
Then I was out of my head
for a week.

MT. HOPE
— for R. P. Dickey

When you shoot me,
shoot me full
of novocaine.
Pain, I'm afraid,
is not my pleasure.
— I've had a dozen
shots before the roots
of the wisdom tooth
were left unusual.
— I've had a toe
dug into
by a pleasant doctor's hand.
He didn't understand because
he wasn't there.
— I must forgive myself
for taking care of me.
I know we measure
life by pain,
but we do, too, by pleasure.

My father locked a door. It was thick oak.
And soft behind the stop I heard them cry:
Not ladies in silk petticoats, and vain,
Nor gentlemen who weep too easily.
Beyond protecting wood I heard a sound
That did not care for me — nor mind to die.
It was the voice my father made, with all
The grace and ease I never understood.
That door is locked: my father could not lie.

Ladies, she said, and gentlemen never chew gum.
Ladies never whistle, she said, nor do gentlemen hum.
I think of this these million miles away
In time. I check the Birmingham Airport sky. What would she say
About the jet Electra there
Rubbing its nose to the wind ? Or care?
She who would not go up — nor near water — and not into
    Mammoth Cave!
Still, she checked off the ones who would, and gave
Each one his check, against or for
His valor, but not in terms of water or wings or caves or even war.
Rather, in terms of chewing gum, of saying thank you please,
Of whistling — these
Were her tests of whether man defied the dust or not.
Indecorous, he might fly to the moon and come back, and still rot.

I go back to him, mottled, stung with bees,
Dragoned by Time's inquisitions.
He was humorous, and he set a graceful table.
He threatened, "I'll make you plunder the tops of trees."
I was always spoiled, but tolerable.
At praying time I sank to my knees
Like a football player, nearly unbearable,
Before an old man's gentle inquisitions.
He prayed. I held to apple trees.

Certain as the mare my father gave me,
Certain as the country, winding ride
Across the afternoon, was that small time
Of quiet which I knew each night before
My father said goodnight and turned from me.

I remember one green afternoon
Of summer when I rode my mare. We crossed
The Old Pike's Bridge, and down below I saw
A car-top. Only that above the water.
I rode away from it into the hills.

After I had put the mare away,
Had eaten supper and undressed for bed,
My father came to me and then I told
About the car. And he made certainty
That hour, and let me sleep with his goodnight.

PART TWO

Imaginary voyages, over the blue brilliance
of glossy paper, do not interest me.
The gray-haired lady at the travel agency
may keep her splashy folders of romance.
I have no longing for camels, Hilton hotels
in unpronounceable countries, sherbets in the desert.
There are always lice and bed bugs. Probably the wells
are dry. Some hard ancient hurt in a peasant's eye
will be too much of right here
to make me sweat in my mind
to trek over there.

Henry Gentle, bloated with too much butter
And sugar on biscuits at breakfast and supper,
Talked about the Bible the way you'd talk
About it if you wrote it.
He'd lean on the mantel or sit
On his cane-bottom chair
And carouse with the angels and devils and afternoon air
In his antique, hightower parlor.
Nothing belied his purity but his color,
Which was red, red
As a young cock's comb.
He spoke of disaster gingerly. At home
He was against picture shows.
Down town, he was against Hitler and loved Roosevelt.
All the time though, bless his heart, he had a wide old belt
That diminished and diminished.
When I see his impromptu grave now where he's finished
His obese talking
I know angels want to be garrulous and temporal and sing.

ZONE OF QUIET DESPERATION
—headline from *Saturday Review*,
October 10, 1964

I won't confess anything —
to sweetheart or priest or friend.
I've got a man stored inside
to the terrible end.
                    He listens
and won't talk back.
But he's a damn sore tooth,
a heart attack, a loss of breath . . .
He's — what can I tell you? —
the dreary end
of the benefit.
He's when you're sober.
He's the imperative.

I've had my fortune told
and all that jazz,
I've been talked to by the fuzz,
I've been to my own particular Alcatraz.
So let it cool.
This isn't wool in my ear.
This is a hearing aid.

SCALOPUS AQUATICUS

Moles yearning like submarines,
Whispering to the earthen seas,
Careening with the roots of roses,
Tunneling, tunneling,
Weeping from blind eyes . . .

    I have seen red roses wither
    Not from the oven sun
    Not from thirst for water
    Not from saintliness

We must have wanderers,
Our stranger-devourers
Munching leaves,
Our greeny aphids, tough cicadas,
Hoboes, monks, bus-stop winos
Drinking the wind's strong alcohol.

Eyes steeped in fur,
No neck to deviate from paths
With grass-root hangings;
Mouse-colored prophet
Dragging a naked tail;

Courier of vibrations,
Silent, wistful prophet:
Guide me with your grass-sick
Mounds of baking earth.
Take me to arrival.

The father speaks:
By its eyes and by the somber tone of its cheeks,
We have known for almost three weeks,
Its mother and I,
That our screaming child is a lie —
Carefully, wrathfully made.

We question the shade
We drew, against the afternoon light . . .
If we had waited till only the beginning of night,
Perhaps, and not
Let go at five o'clock the hot . . .

From here on: as we lie apart,
Sleeping and waking our separate ways, each heart
Will beat a separate path
Back to its own wrath.

He tells her: "See,
The violet blooms from
The dead pig's ear.
The sun doesn't care.
The bee doesn't care;
It circles and darts,
Flusters the air
Till it's satisfied."

He pulls a violet and says:
"Wear this in your hair."

She moves away and says:
"Once my mind is fixed
It's staid. I could take
That violet to an oak tree
Shade, watch it strengthen
In the cool — but I am a fool.
I would remember a dead pig's ear.
When you spoke pretty words
I would not hear you.
I would not kiss you.
I would be afraid."

He dropped the violet and said:
"We'll leave this to the dead."
And they did and they walked to the shade.

ENEMY CAMP

I'm afraid I've reckoned with
the enemy camp —
and loved it there.
Where is a chair so beautiful

as the one you'll break?
I've talked for days
with the poisonous snake
who leans hard on his venom.

Yes, I was afraid.
But what went on between us
in that glade,
where we sought each other out —

that was something to talk about.

I saw you in my room last night,
Ugly as yesterday.
I saw you this morning, caught by the bright
Sunshine.

Just now as I dine,
Supposedly alone, you
Sit across the booth,
Arrogant as anyone who

Is taking control.
I saw you in the window at Scruggs',
A mannequin wearing mink.
Even through glass, buster! I could smell your stink.

DOG DAYS
—It is said that the Englishman Kim Philby,
who defected to Russia, had nightmares and
stuttered in his sleep.

Cannister is scouring out
His mother's kitchen sink.
His mother's gone a week.
Besides, the TV broke.

Rocks turn their backs.
They echo heat.
Worms scream and dig deeper.
Where has the single red bird gone
That was here in July?

Cannister has taken sleeping pills.
He won't awaken till it's dark.
The windows in his room are shut.
His underwear is sweaty.

Where do things go?
North Pole is too far.
The sun is slow, slow.
The river stops to rot.

Sometimes it's morning.
Cannister won't dress.
The postman makes his yearly round.
Cannister has sent a card.

While a squat pine tree
Drinks up dry earth,
And bitterweed is the flower,
Boys can't play barefoot in the dew.
— *It's the dog days, that's who*!

    A week has gone, a day.
    Cannister won't pray.
    He stutters in his sleep.
    He won't eat a bite.

Heat lightning forms the distance.
It is game to be deluded.
Loves that lasted the shaggy ice
Are concluded.
Ducks are cross with pebbles.

    One morning they will find her.
    An alley in a city.
    Her bashed-in head still bleeding.
    Cannister won't care.

The crop over there, over there,
Over there:
Somewhere rain is falling.
Blue gills search the murkiest deeps.
Nobody thinks of roses.

EICHMANN IN JERUSALEM
        —after reading Hannah Arendt

   We must presuppose ourselves.
Die at our own hands.
(Stupidity can be
lyrical. But there's no lyric
in this solemn German whisper.)
We can set the monster
by a standard. How can we set
the less than ordinary head?

There's something outside the law that might be worse
Than the jury's sentence of Finality:
Mother gone and Father gone; a hearse
To wobble you on the cliff, over the sea.

What happens when the bandages are gone?
When the wounds are tender yet, and sometimes bleed?
You sit upon the cyanidal throne,
Ask for a mercy even the stars won't read.

You breathe a curse to an elemental dark,
Deform your head by raising it too high.
There's comfort in the belly of the shark.
He's not for the likes of you! Let him go by!

do the walls relax,
do their violent red flowers fade
together, making a kind of
pleasant hell
to be surrounded by?

Does the novel's prose
go smoother than it did?
And is the hop-head hero
more like a friend or accomplice
or enemy?

Yes.
But tomorrow, black coffee,
the stripping off of vanity,
the cooling off,
one must remain at least partially true:
accomplice, friend, enemy.

IN THE RED

Q.: Why do elephants drink?
A.: To forget.

I see the herd of them — their ragged skin
Warring against the formal afternoon sky —
As they sit, like lumps, for cocktails to begin.
"I think back on each conjugal lie

I've told," they wheeze; and this is their party talk.
Their skin goes red from gray as the sun descends.
"Wouldn't it be tranquility-grand to walk
Innocent at dawn, fresh, and at loose ends?"

They drink themselves ad nauseum till three,
When a cynical moon throws a little light, to lunge home.
Guilty insomniacs in their misery
They squint, all trembling, into the jungle, alone.

Frank, the mongrel dog, and I —
we have mange together. I with
my dandruff and flaking face,
Frank with his thinning hair and sores.
 — Old wanderer, dear tramp, and evil-smelling
wagger-of-tail, he almost blesses me
when I break out the canned horse meat.
 But I am Frank's defeat.
The mange won't cure: I kill him.
 Who is my defeat? To give me
mercy I don't want.

THE HEREFORD BULL AT DAWN

The Hereford bull —
His underside low to the ground —
Munches till his belly is full,
And makes little sound.

And he will not eat too much.
He minds his girth.
Vanity, as such,
Arrived at birth.

A pasture backs him up.
Beyond the pasture, trees.
And more beyond, a sun comes up
As if to please

The Hereford bull.
There's elegance in his stance
As he eats till his belly is full,
With never a side glance.

Aristocratic ton,
Garlanded with pride,
He moves away from everyone
With everyone at his side.

Rimbaud, demented, the angry child,
Stamping his peasant feet at the wind,
Wept later when the weather was mild
And he was motherless and with no friend.

Summers teach us strange declensions,
Drive us from home, then drive us back;
The very best of our final intentions
May leave our minds demoniac.

Even money, father of all,
When father has left on a virile pursuit,
Only exclaims the frightening pall
Of a handsome face gone irresolute.

The money is safe and will not rust
But cancer is moving upward always.
There is nothing the wavering eyes can trust
When dementia returns on the final days.

"A chocolate-brown, full breast is worth
All of your money, most of your mirth."

Gauguin, surrounded by red trees,
Said this in order to appease

His empty stomach and his pride.
Proud, empty, Gauguin died.

FOR MARY LOU WILLIAMS, AT PIANO, AT THE HICKORY HOUSE

Not one for schmaltz, not for moxie;
And I cannot improve her
In poetry: her fingers black
And growing to the ivory keys
And to the black: her wide eyes
Closed.

— My heart and head reach out.
I think of a dark madonna without child.
Behind her, two dark wise men, bass and drummer,
Beat out their adoration.

BE GENTLE
    — for John Crowe Ransom

With ironies of tenses and inversions,
Meanderings through a green fabulous garden,
Snap us to appropriate conversions!
Sir, begging your pardon.

Tell us more the color blue will fail,
Girls must ever leave their summer places.
It is our minds, not we, are frail.
Minds, more than faces.

Though we must be reminded of the flowers,
Nudged to notice Death's precise invasions,
Be gentle when you tell us that our hours
Are bony bleak equations.

FOR MAXWELL BODENHEIM

Who you spoke to —
"His voice like jewels
dropped in a satin bag" —
didn't care for the bragging
at the marketplace. Rather
nobody cared, not even
the gimleted hooded
somebody else in the bar
where you warred over
doggerel
for a cheap drink, stiff
enough for angels.
— Yours were the golden locks
gone lice.
In your room
with the psycho
and the beat-up whore
they found her blood and yours
sweet to the melted air.
The Sea Around Us
lay open somewhere
on the floor.

I WOULD HAVE THE MIND . . .

There are many wanderings
the mind takes,
subtle and leaf-shadowed paths,
blocked with sudden things
impossible to define:
a branch that rakes
the face of the mind
as it goes those paths.

I would not change a night of a day
when the mind goes astray.
I would have its face so lashed
nothing could erase
the bleeding.

THAT'S MY BOY

My God if I ever hear
another father
at another liquor luncheon
(whiskey sour and/or martini)
in a dinky hotel
announce how his son did
in High football . . .
— I mean, how he did
that night
when Scooter was playing too.
Who's Scooter the hell?
He's something for fathers
and mothers
to live on —
the way they live on
their ineffectual boy
whose future ended
two years ago
and who will soon be
in the employ
of I.B.M.
— His hair, oh Lord, is
miraculously parted.

THE MATING AND DYING OF A FLY

Go away, go away,
and I don't give a damn,
not a bloody,
about your dung-sprung children.
It's time for frost
and time to get lost
the way my children are
and my friends.

Go away, go away,
and whatever April sunny day
don't come back!
Step on a crack
before you spawn!
Let us yawn
without your intrusion.

They plant me here on this screwball porch.
The door is locked and I can't shave. But the moon
comes up. I stare it back as long as I can.
The sun hurts my eyes. Who can rock to Bethlehem?
     — They all go away. I want to go.
        I take my head in my hands like this
        and I ram my head and I ram my head
        till all the flies fly away.
Oh, the people come back. I know they will.
They put a lizard in my head. It scrambles around
for a little while, till they go away, then I go away.
We do it every day.

                    There was
expensive caviar, and
there was whatever you wanted
at a portable bar.
— But I was beside myself,
thinking of cages for lions
and lions out of cages.

But I think I drank too literally,
and the host and hostess,
squirming a little, did their best
not to believe me.

MY LADY OF THE BLACK RAINCOAT

I.

I light a cigarette and see by the flame
it's two o'clock. Where are you tonight?
Whose blood are you sucking? Who do you mount?
    — Last night when it rained
      you came to my window,
      and I let you in.
                    Naked
      beneath the black raincoat
      you lay beside me and fed
      me sleeping pills. And then
      you left. Where did you go?
      This morning they pumped my stomach.
      Why did you leave me?

II.

Sometime come to me
when the sky is June
and birds are blue
and red on the grass,
when there is an oak
tree moving with wind.
Then let me see your face,
my love. For once, out
of shadows. For once, by day.
This is a dare.

III.

You are My Lady of the Soot,
of the Spider's Belly, of the
Wild Pig's Squeal.
                    My wrist
against the razor blade
tells me you're as real as
nausea and delirium and
electric shock racing the bones.
You're My Lady of the Stones,
My Lady of Dry Spittle,
of the Black Raincoat,
of Despair.

The headache that arises with you
from your bed, that has sprawled
in your dreams, and goes with you
to your morning coffee cup, and after —
you have called it from somewhere to be with you.
We do. We perfect our failures with pain,
not consciously always, not heroically always,
but sometimes heroically we call for pain
to let us know what heroism is, or failure is —
or wrong: what's death, forewarned by pain.

A diversion in North Alabama:
my love under a pear tree
in bloom, and my love
smoking Old Golds,
and saying, needlessly, she
will be my love forever.
— A striking and therapeutic
diversion, we, most of us,
need: more beautiful
than alcohol, more tender and
golden; and for a month
much more loving . . .
— But nevertheless, like
sailboats, off from the shore
where you're sitting:
a finely tinted diversion.
(Something to take your attention
from dry crops behind you
and the cities drowned in July heat.)

Your eyes are usually wide awake and there are usually
Dracula-black half-circles under them. They are not
very interesting eyes. I can read too well what's behind
them. I can even see the particular hells that have
been submerged to give you such celluloid eyes. The
pity of it is: neither George Raft nor Edward G.
Robinson caused those eyes to be — much less Bugsy or
Dutch or Al. They register minor dooms and ugly wisdom.

A WISH

I must know the exact eye
of the exact creature; color
going too red in the cheek.
A tear rather than dolor.

And the exact hair,
even if dyed,
touching my cheek and shoulder.
Nothing implied!